How would we live in a world without

PINK?

by

Mishiemashy

For Ruth

This book belong to

....

....

....

Imagine a world without a trace of pink, Where roses are red, but some fade to brink.
Cherry blossoms bloom in shades not found, A soft blush lost, no petals around.

Sunsets would lack that rosy hue,
A colder sky, less warm to view.
No dawn's blush across morning's face,
Just reds and golds in pink's empty space.

Without pink, flamingos turn pale and meek,
Their feathers washed, no colors peak.
The coral reefs lose a vibrant hue,
Fading to shadows in deeper blue.

Cotton candy would miss its shade so sweet,
Just wisps of white, not quite complete.
A carnival treat, but lacking cheer,
Without pink's warmth to draw it near.

The flush in cheeks when we feel shy,
Would cool to beige, not quite as spry.
No rosy glow when love is near, Just
muted tones, less warm and dear.

No pink balloons to float and sway,
Just blues and greens to mark the day.
Birthday parties lose their spark,
No pink to light up the park.

The springtime blooms, once fresh and bright,
Would lack that rosy, gentle light.
Magnolias pale, hibiscus plain,
A softer world lost in the rain.

Ribbons and bows with colors bright,
Would lack that hue that brings delight.

No pink to soften edges sharp,
A harsher world, a colder spark.

The blushing dusk, so soft, so fair,
Would feel less warm, no pinks to share.
A sunset cooled, a lost embrace,
No pink in twilight's sweet grace.

The color of hope in ribbons worn,
Would fade away, no pink adorned.
A world less bright in causes fought,
Where pink once stood, now empty thought.

The gentle warmth in twilight's face,
Would miss that glow in quiet space.
The day would end in darker shade,
As pinkless nights would softly fade.

The sweets we savor—no pink delight,
Just yellows and greens in every bite.
No pink frosting to crown a cake, Just
neutrals now, and hearts that ache.

Piglets born with coats of light,
Would be plain white, a pale sight.
Farmyards lacking that gentle hue,
A softer world we'd bid adieu.

Our world of art with colors wide,
Would miss pink's warmth, hard to hide.
The soft and bold would seem less
real, No pink to lift what we feel.

Pink lemonade would simply fade,
No cheerful tint, just yellow made.
A duller sip on summer's day, With
pink erased, it's less than play.

No pink in seashells on the shore,
Just whites and creams and nothing more.
No blush in sand where waters play,
A world of gray in dawn's display.

In fashion's world, no pink attire,
Just shades of green that soon tire.
No bubblegum tops or pastel trend,
The pinkless wardrobe we can't defend.

Cherry ice cream no longer sweet,
Just cream and red in melted beat.
The shades of pink that flavors bring,
Would be no more, a missing thing.

No pink glow in a gentle flush,
Just muted hues, a faded blush.
The warmth of joy that pink imparts,
Would leave a chill on tender hearts.

In roses, coral, skies, and cheeks,
A missing hue in nature speaks.
A world of color less complete,
With pink erased, the loss replete.

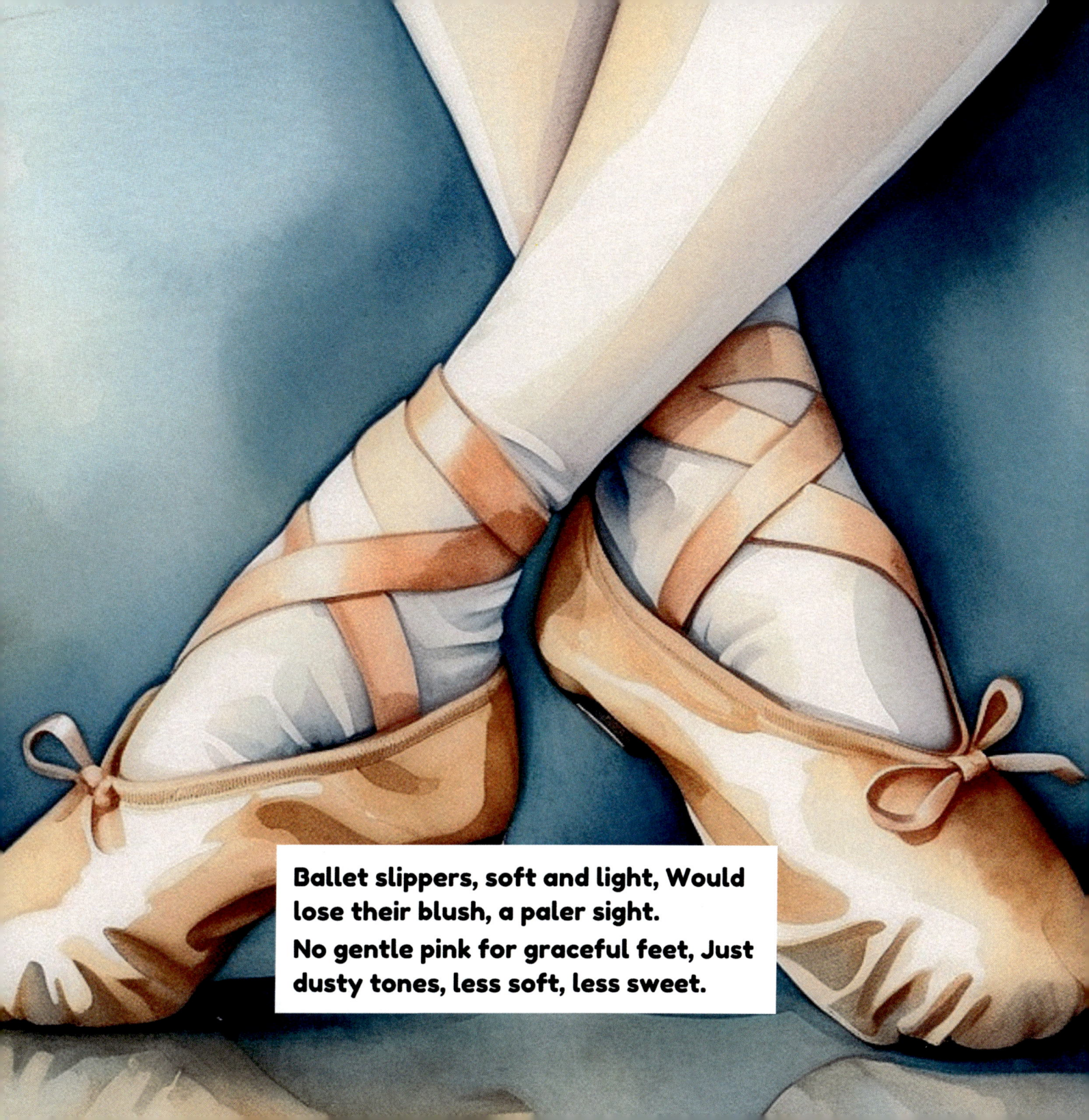

Ballet slippers, soft and light, Would lose their blush, a paler sight.
No gentle pink for graceful feet, Just dusty tones, less soft, less sweet.

Peonies and tulips lose their charm,
Gardens feel cold, lacking warm.

A duller world without that glow,
The floral scene would feel too low.

A strawberry's hue would lose its flair,
A duller red, not quite as rare.

The juicy fruit would lose its blush,
Less vibrant red, a simple hush.

Cherry blossoms without their blush,
A muted white, a simple hush.
Spring's celebration less alive,
Without pink's hue, hard to survive.

No pink horizon as daylight wanes,
Just purples and reds in winding chains.
The dawn's sweet blush would not
appear, A world without pink, less near.

Hearts on cards for Valentine's day,
Would miss the shade that lights the way.
Just reds and whites to show we care,
With pink no longer present there.

In every rainbow's arching glow,
Pink would be missed from nature's show.
A softer note in colors bright,
Erased from day, erased from night.

The playful blush of youth's own face,
Would fade away, a colder space.
No pink to paint the joy of life, Just
gray and red, less soft, less rife.

So cherish pink in all you see,
A hue of warmth, of joy, of glee.
For if it's gone, our world grows small,
With pink we feel, with pink we fall.

We hope you enjoyed "How Would We Live in a World Without PINK?" ✦ Discover more exciting books in the "How would we live in a world without... ?" series. If you loved this book, don't forget to share it with friends and inspire even more readers! ♥ Together, let's keep wondering, learning, and exploring! ✦ Stay curious, because the world is full of questions waiting to be answered! ✦

Happy reading,
Mishiemashy

Your feedback really makes a world of difference.

Please leave a review on Amazon.

Made in the USA
Monee, IL
27 March 2025

14741362R00021